MW01298197

Kuwait Travel Guide.

Tourism

Author
Jesse Russell.

Publisher:
SONITTEC LTD
College House, 2nd
Floor
17 King Edwards
Road,
Ruislip
London
HA4 7AE .

Table of Content

Summary

How Traveling Can Broaden Your Perspective

Kuwait Tour: You may not need a lot of convincing when it comes to finding a reason to travel especially when considering a trip to a foreign country. Exploring the world, seeing new places, and learning about new cultures are just a few of the benefits of traveling. There is value to exploring someplace new and combating the stress of getting out of your comfort zone.

Traveling should be looked at as a journey for personal growth, mental health, and spiritual enlightenment. Taking the time to travel to a new place can both literally and figuratively open your eyes to things you have never seen before. These new experiences allow you to get to know yourself in ways you can't if you stay in the same place.

- ✓ Traveling is wonderful in so many ways:

- ✓ You can indulge your sense of wanderlust.

- ✓ You experience different cultures.

- ✓ Your taste buds get to experience unique foods.

- ✓ You meet all different kinds of people.

As you grow older, your mind evolves and expands to adapt to the new information you receive. Traveling to a new destination is similar in this way, but the learning process occurs at a faster rate. Traveling thrusts you into the unknown and delivers you with a bounty of new information and ideas. The expansion of your mind is one of the greatest benefits of travel. Keep reading to learn six more benefits of traveling.

> Discover Your Purpose: Feeling as though you have a purpose in life is more important than many people realize. A purpose connects you to something bigger than yourself and keeps you moving forward. Your purpose in life can change suddenly and fluidly as you enter new stages in becoming who you are. With each new stage in life, there comes new goals and callings. Traveling can help open your eyes to a new life direction. You may be wandering down a path unaware of where you will end up. Seeing new places and meeting new people can help you break from that path and discover what your true purpose is.

Traveling is an excellent remedy for when you feel you need to refocus on your purpose and goals, or re-evaluate your life path. There is no better time to open your eyes than when your life seems to be out of focus and in need of redirection. You might just be surprised by what you discover and find a new sense of life purpose how traveling changes you.

Traveling is a way to discover parts of yourself that you never knew existed. While traveling, you have no choice but to deal with unexpected situations. For example, how you may typically handle a problem at home might be a completely unacceptable approach when you are in an unfamiliar place without all of the comforts and conveniences of home.

> Be Aware of Your Blessings: When you travel to a new destination, your eyes are opened to new

standards, and, you become more aware of all the blessings and privileges you have been given. It is easy to forget what you do have and only focus on what is missing from your life. Traveling can help put things back into perspective and re-center your priorities on what truly matters.

Consider traveling through an area that has no electricity or running water if you come from a place where cold bottled water is easily accessible and nearly anything you want can be delivered to your door in less than an hour. These are two completely different worlds and ways of living. For people who experience a more privileged quality of life, seeing others who live in drastically different situations can help you appreciate what you have and spark an interest for you to lend support to people living elsewhere.

> Find Truth: There's concept, and then there's experience. You can know things from reading them online and listening to a lecture, but to experience something in person is different.

Traveling can help open your eyes to the true kindness and goodness of humanity. There is a myth that when you travel you are on your own, but that simply is not the case. The welcoming attitude and overwhelming hospitality that people give to travelers may be one of the most surprising truths about traveling. Beyond that, you have the whole world to learn about with every place you discover, through every person you meet and every culture you experience.

> Expand Your Mind: A key benefit of traveling, or taking the opportunity to explore on a vacation, is being given the opportunity to expand your mind in ways you can't imagine. If

you can allow yourself to travel with an open mind and accept the new experiences and adventures around you, you give your mind the chance to see the world from a new perspective.

Think of it as a spiritual and intellectual enlightenment. You never stop being curious and should always seek out education whenever possible throughout your life. You are doing a disservice to yourself if you choose to close yourself off from the world. It is not always easy to let new ideas in, especially when they are in direct contrast with what you may believe. You have everything you need to grow, you just have to allow yourself to do it.

> Connect to Others: It's easy to forget how similar you are to others, regardless of where you come from, what your background is, or how much money you have. At the end of the day,

human beings share more in common with one another than they may choose to admit. When taking a trip to a different country, you may have learned to cast aside what is different and unusual because from the outside, others may not look or act alike. But if you give yourself a chance, you may be surprised to find how minimal and superficial these differences are.

As you notice how you share similar needs, your perspective of your home expands, you become friends with people from different backgrounds and cultures, you realize how everyone is connected. This state of awareness is a jump in consciousness that can help you experience a world-centric view of consciousness more expansive and aware.

> Break Out of Your Shell: Without a doubt, one of the benefits of traveling is that it forces you to

step out of your bubble, which can provide you with many emotional health benefits. Yes, it may be uncomfortable and scary to break away from your daily routine, but the rewards are worth it. What you gain in experience and knowledge may outweigh any amount of doubt or apprehension you had before embarking on your journey. Travel also helps you to self-reflect and dig deep into who you are as a person.

Something magical happens when people are put in new situations than they are normally faced with in their everyday life, as behavior becomes more raw and real as a result of being out of your conditioned environment. This not-so-subtle push into the world helps you to become more open and comfortable expressing yourself without the worry of feeling judged.

> See the Big Picture: Life is a limited gift. You must choose to make the most of each day. As you travel and experience more of the world, you may be struck with gratitude and appreciation for all the places you have enjoyed and people you've shared your travels with. You have the power to take control of your life and can inspire you to start doing more.

About Kuwait

Kuwait Introduction

Kuwait is a country of the Arabian Peninsula located in the northwestern corner of the Persian Gulf.

A small emirate nestled between Iraq and Saudi Arabia, Kuwait is situated in a section of one of the driest, least-hospitable deserts on Earth. Its shore, however, includes Kuwait Bay, a deep harbour on the Persian Gulf. There, in the 18th century, Bedouin from the interior founded a trading post. The name *Kuwait* is derived from the Arabic diminutive of the Hindustani *kūt* ("fort"). Since the emirate's ruling family, the Āl

Ṣabāḥ, formally established a sheikhdom in 1756, the country's fortunes have been linked to foreign commerce. In time and with accumulated wealth, the small fort grew to become Kuwaitcity, a modern metropolis mingling skyscrapers, apartment buildings, and mosques. Kuwait city has most of the country's population, which makes Kuwait one of the world's most-urbanized countries.

The tiny country, which was a British protectorate from 1899 until 1961, drew world attention in 1990 when Iraqi forces invaded and attempted to annex it. A United Nationscoalition led by the United States drove Iraq's army out of Kuwait within days of launching an offensive in February 1991, but the retreating invaders looted the country and set fire to most of its oil wells (*see* Persian Gulf War). Kuwait has largely recovered from the effects of the war and again has one of the highest per capita incomes in the world. Its generally conservative government continues to provide generous material benefits for Kuwaiti citizens, and, though conservative elements in its society resisted such reforms as women's suffrage (women were not enfranchised until 2005), it has remained relatively stable. It has been called an "oasis" of peace and safety amid an otherwise turbulent region.

The Beauty of the Nation

In Kuwait you'll find an intriguing mix of Western liberalism and traditional Islamic culture. The capital, Kuwait City, is a bustling metropolis of high-rise buildings and luxury hotels, while the Gulf country is also home to spectacular mosques and palaces. Religion is an integral part of daily life here.

This juxtaposition perhaps stems from Kuwait's marrying of Islamism with oil wealth, which for decades has earned it the attention of Western powers. Upon independence from Britain in 1961, Sheikh Abdullah assumed head of state, adopting the title of emir. The large revenues from oil production allowed independent Kuwait to build up its economic infrastructure and institute educational and social welfare programmes.

In the early 1990s, the emir established a National Assembly (*Majlis*), which placed limits on the power of the ruling family. Since then, the national assembly has clashed several times with the emir and the cabinet (which is still dominated by the al-Sabah family) over misuse of state funds and poor management of the all-important oil industry. Underlying these disputes is the growing impression that the ageing al-

Sabah clan is no longer capable of running the country. However, they continue to dominate Kuwaiti policies.

Surrounded by three major Middle Eastern powers, Kuwait became the target of Iraqi territorial claims, leading to Saddam Hussein's invasion of the country in 1990. The Kuwaitis later recovered their country by virtue of a US-led, UN-backed multinational military force.

After a period of euphoria, the Kuwaitis had to address a number of difficult questions; the future security of the country was dealt with by the signing of defence and security pacts with the USA, the UK and Kuwait's Gulf allies. More recently, Kuwait was one of the first countries to join Operation Iraqi Freedom following the US-led war against Iraq, and provided aid and support during Iraq's (ongoing) process of reconstruction.

Beyond the geopolitical dimension, Kuwait is a fascinating country with much elaborate architecture and a superb culinary tradition. Its inhabitants are a warm, welcoming bunch, while the fact that Kuwait is a bit less glitzy than other oil-rich Gulf countries means that it can feel like a haven of tradition Arab culture.

Country guide

Sightseeing
Kuwait sightseeing. Travel guide attractions, sights, nature and touristic places

In the past, Kuwait had to undergo tough war times, but nowadays it's a peaceful country, which billion dollar oil industry allowed performing of a massive restoration and building modern metropolises. Nowadays, the country attracts numerous travelers who come to rest on Failaka Island, discover sights of Kuwait City and enjoy spectacular beach rest.

Scuba diving and snorkeling become increasingly popular in Kuwait. In order to make underwater life even more picturesque, many coral reefs are being restored in the country. Even without diving, beautiful white sand beaches are very captivating, so rest in one of numerous resorts of the country will leave many pleasant memories.

Kuwait Towers have quickly become a symbol of Kuwait City, the capital of the country. The three towers were finished in 1979. The main tower is 187m high and is open for visitors. There are an observation deck and a restaurant at the height of 123 meters; the tower rotates slowly and makes a full circle in 30 minutes. The other two towers are used to store water for emergency needs and control electricity. Kuwait Towers were damaged severely during the war, but were restored later.

Salmiya and Hawalli are considered the main residential and business parts of the city. The Science Center located in Salmiya is a great place to visit for both adults and children. The center is located near the waterfront and a beautiful marina. As-Seef Palace and Bayan Palace are considered the most beautiful palaces in the city. The first palace is one of the residences of the Emir, while the second one is used as the government quarters.

There are some attractions outside Kuwait City as well. Jal Az-Zor Nature Reserve, which is located not far away from the capital, is a great place to see migratory birds. Some of the birds like Black Vulture are very rare and nearly impossible to see in other parts of the world. Other famous nature reserves in the country are Sulaibikhat Bay, Dawhat Kazima, Al-Jahra Pools Nature Reserve, Ad-Doha Nature Reserve and Coral Islets. Travellers are also welcome to explore the desert and see wild animals there.

Kuwait is a popular destination for shopping fans. Giant shopping malls, walking streets with various shops, finest jewellery stores and trendy boutiques will certainly make hearts of fashionista beat faster.

History and Entertainment
Kuwait is one of the youngest countries in the world. It was formed in the 18th century. The founders of the country are representatives of the Bedouin tribe coming to the territory of the present country from the shores of the Persian Gulf. The country was located at the crossroads

of important trade routes that caused its rapid and successful development.

Kuwait quickly became one of the largest suppliers of coffee, spices and pearls in the world. Another important activity here was the breeding of thoroughbred horses. Since its formation, the new country was officially a part of the Ottoman Empire. For many years, it saw multiple wars between Turks and Britons for its territory. When the Ottoman Empire fell in 1899, Kuwait became a British protectorate.

The boundaries of the country were finally formed only in 1927 and still remain unchangeable. The country gained independence from Great Britain only in 1961. In 1991, Kuwait managed to break free from the Iraqi protectorate. Nowadays, the country is one of the best places in the world for acquainting with Arab culture and traditions.

Cities and regions

Kuwait City
Guide to Kuwait City
Sightseeing in Kuwait City what to see.
Complete travel guide
Kuwait (El Kuwait) is the capital of Kuwait located on the southern bank of Kuwait Bay (a part of the Persian Gulf). This is the largest port of the country. The population of the city estimates 32.4 thousands of people as for 2005. This is the only large megalopolis on the country.

For a long time Kuwait was powered mostly by fishing, pearl fishery and well-developed trading relations with India and East Africa. After the end of World War II oil production started in Kuwait, quickly turning it into a large megalopolis. Today in Kuwait are well-developed such areas as food, cement, and petrochemical industries; machine building, consumer electronics manufacturing, ship repairs and ship building. The city is also famous by the only in the country and the largest in the world water desalinization factory and pearl fishing. Kuwait is also an important transport and trading crossing.

The architecture of Kuwait has suffered severely from the war with Iraq. That's why the center of the city is full of modern buildings and only in the suburbs of Kuwait one can see old one-storey wattle and daub buildings. The center of the city is the location of the official residence of emir, various governmental facilities that border with luxurious mansions that belong to the high class of the country. If you make a walk on Fahd Al Salem Street, you will see numerous trading centers, banks and comfortable hotels. All buildings here are very tall and are not very different comparing to architecture of European countries.

Main sights of Kuwait include the main mosque, Sief Palace, the Tareq Rajab Museum, and Kuwait Towers Skyscrapers. You can also visit the National Museum, where you can find archeological findings and a large ethnographic exposition. Your visit to Museum of Islamic Arts will be no less interesting. Failaka Island that is located not far away from the city is the location of another sight the ruins of the Greek Temple built in IV century.

Kuwait is famous for its luxurious skyscrapers. One of the most beautiful is Al-Hamra. This 77-storey skyscraper is one of the highest in the world. Within its walls, there is a lot of entertainment for tourists. Here is a popular shopping center, various cinemas and a sports club, and on the roof of the skyscraper is located one of the most luxurious and expensive restaurants in the capital.

Fans of unusual excursions will be invited to visit the ancient vessel Al Hashemi II, which can be seen on the waterfront. This ship is a record holder of the Guinness Book of Records. It is the largest ship on the planet, completely built of wood. The length of the ship is 100 meters, and it weighs about 2,500 tons. For tourists, there are interesting excursions, and on board the ship there is a posh restaurant where only the wealthiest citizens and guests of Kuwait can afford to dine.

One of the main symbols of Kuwait is the Musical Fountain, which is one of the largest in the world. In fact, it is a huge complex consisting of 220 fountains and three huge pools. Around the fountains there is an incredibly beautiful recreation area with benches and playgrounds for children. It is most interesting to relax in this place in the evening when the fountains are decorated with luxurious illumination.

The most interesting architectural monument is the Emir Old Seif Palace. It is a real oriental palace, built in accordance with all national traditions. The main feature of the building is a graceful turret with a beautiful clock. Very beautiful ceramic tiles and natural gold were used with its decoration.

In another remarkable building, which can also be considered a model of national architecture, there is the Tareq Rajab Museum. Within its walls is a rich collection of works of art and objects of calligraphy. The founder of this museum is a couple from Kuwait who have devoted their entire lives to scientific work. Recently, the collection of the museum was replenished with unique products made of ceramics, as well as ancient weapons and jewelry. The couple collected this unique collection all their life. The museum exhibits are brought from various Arab countries. The museum's collection is constantly replenished, so it will be interesting to visit even for those who have already visited this beautiful mansion.

Family trip with kids

Family trip to Kuwait City with children. Ideas on where to go with your child

In Kuwait, tourists with children should definitely visit the local Kuwait Zoo. It is located on the territory of an incredibly beautiful park, in which there are artificial lakes with swans. Animals in this zoo stroll along spacious enclosures. In this zoo, you can see rare predators including brown bears and lions. Among the friendliest inhabitants, it is worth noting giraffes and gazelles who gladly accept treats from visitors. The zoo is quite large, and it will be nice to take a walk in it on a sunny day, and relax in the shade of trees.

Among the amusement parks in Kuwait, KidZania deserves top priority. This entertainment center is indoors and is located in one of the city's largest shopping and entertainment centers. Children here are offered to take a ride on a small bright train. There is also an interesting children's playground and various game simulators in the center. Nearby, there are many interesting shops designed for children, as well as cozy cafes with a wide selection of sweets.

There is a beautiful water park in the city, which is sure to appeal to water enthusiasts. This water park is quite old, but has everything for an interesting holiday: large pools with slides, comfortable terraces with sun loungers and parasols, and a cafe with a large selection of soft drinks and popular dishes.

For many travelers with children, the amusement park Kuwait Entertainment City is most popular. It is a large beautiful park with many bright landscapes, sculptures and attractions. The main advantage of the park is that many of its attractions and playgrounds can be used by visitors for free. There are many beautiful fountains in the park, and outfitted convenient walking paths. Game rooms and attractions obtainable in the park are designed for children from two years of age.

With older children, it is worth looking into the entertainment center - The Scientific Center. As you can guess by its name, this complex introduces young guests to the achievements of modern science, and also presents an interesting collection of natural science exhibits to visitors. In the museum, visitors can see fragments of skeletons of prehistoric animals. On the territory of the center, there is also a small aquarium. Visitors to the center will be able to see mock-ups of old ships and wooden boats that locals used hundreds of years ago. The scientific center is incredibly interesting. Both children and adults will learn a lot of new things in it.

The city has a reasonable choice of parks, so nature enthusiasts also do not have to search for a suitable place for recreation for a long time. You can have a good time with the whole family in Al Shaheed Park. It has several beautiful miniature lakes with fountains on its territory. Here you can stroll among the exotic trees, feed the birds swimming in the lakes, and enjoy a hassle-free atmosphere. The park is very large, and has sports grounds and special picnic areas on its territory.

It will be interesting to visit the Bayan Botanical Garden with children. Part of its unique collection of plants and flowers is hidden under a huge transparent dome. Here you can see the rarest kinds of exotic plants from around the world. The adjoining territory of the botanical garden is notable for the variety of landscape decorations and fountains in it, next to which, will be pleasant to relax on a hot day.

Culture: sights to visit

Culture of Kuwait City. Places to visit old town, temples, theaters, museums and palaces

Kuwait City is a picturesque place with many monuments, museums and colorful markets, which also have become major tourist attractions. An important tourist landmark is the Kuwait National Museum, which is famous for the collection of objects of Islamic art and priceless archaeological finds. Those, who want to become better acquainted with works of local artists and sculptors, would like the Museum of Islamic Art. The collection of antique furniture and exquisite interior is represented in the Tareg Rajab private museum.

Among the ancient monuments the Al-Khalifa, the construction of which took place in the early 18th century, points out. This beautiful religious building was built keeping best national traditions. Over the years of its existence it has been hit hard, but the surviving building look very impressive. The Great Mosque is the unique construction and the brightest monument of modern architecture. It was completed in 1986.

The area's unique complex is about 50,000 square meters. The minaret is 74 meters height. The mosque is free to take a few thousand people; the unique massive construction is supported by only four pillars.

Some older religious objects, such as the mosque of Ibn al-Hammes and Matabba, have also preserved in Kuwait. Both of them were founded in the 18th century. Today they don't cease to amaze curious travelers with their impressive appearance. Returning to the subject of modern monuments, it is worth mentioning Kuwaiti towers. Beautiful skyscrapers were built in 1979; the height of the largest tower is 187 meters. Tops of skyscrapers are equipped with excellent viewing platforms that are among most popular attractions for tourists.

Excursion to Old Seif Palace will provide an unforgettable experience. It is the most important monument of the late 19th century. Indescribable atmosphere of luxury reigns in palace; its design is fine in every detail and it is entirely consistent with appearance that took place a hundred years ago. Tourists should definitely see surviving fortifications of the city, Shamiyya, Maskab, Baraisi and Jahra gateways. Several centuries ago, Kuwait was a powerful fortress city, in 1957 the surrounding walls were completely destroyed, but gates have managed to preserve to the present day.

Besides mosques, the capital of Kuwait has several Christian churches. First of all, it's worth highlighting the National Evangelical Church known for its spacious interior. Perhaps it is because of this that many representatives from other countries gather here, this is one of the most multicultural places in town, just like the capital of Kuwait is. Another outstanding religious monument is the Holy Family Cathedral Parish, the construction of which coincided with the year when Kuwait gained independence, which happened in 1961. Inside one can find a scaled-down replica of the statue of Our Lady of Arabia, which is a priceless artifact for Christians.

Get acquainted with the colonial period in the life of Kuwait in Dickson House Cultural Center, on the ground floor of which are rooms where the interior of that time has remained virtually untouched. The cultural center is named after Harold Dickson who was a colonel during the period of a British protectorate in Kuwait. In addition to the interior, there are interesting archives and photographs, as well as models of residential areas of the city as they were in the colonial era. All the exhibits date back to the late

19th century and the 60s of the 20th century when Kuwait gained its independence. Of great interest to travelers is another museum - namely, the Amricani Cultural Center. Formerly its building served as an American hospital - that's how Americans helped the local people at the beginning of the 20th century. Besides, it keeps a collection of pearls and ancient artifacts, which will surely impress any visitor.

In Al Qurain Martyrs Museum, one can learn more about the history of Kuwait - in particular, about the tragic events of the 2003 invasion of Iraq. The museum itself is a house that was abandoned immediately after the intervention. Thus, visitors will be able to get a clear picture of what was happening here at that time. For locals, this is a real reminder of rough times and challenges, which they have coped with thanks to their unbreakable spirit and concerted efforts.

Kuwaiti Maritime Museum tells about Kuwait as a maritime country, technology buffs will be amazed by a great collection of ship models. Well, those who are fond of vintage cars (like many emirs of Kuwait whose cars are also included in the collection) will appreciate the exhibits presented in the Historical, Vintage & Classic Car Museum.

A unique of its kind is the Mirror House where visitors can see priceless works of art literally at every step - that is, under their feet. The entire floor and walls are lined with magnificent mosaics, the museum looks more like a palace in which a sultan could live. All tourists are recommended to follow the city's cultural events. Most of the best theatrical performances take place in the Sheikh Jaber Al Ahmad Cultural Center. To find peace of mind and aesthetic enjoyment, it's worth exploring Bayan Botanical

Garden, a green oasis in the desert, which is especially beautiful in the summer and striking with its wonderful aromas in the springtime.

Attractions & nightlife

City break in Kuwait City. Active leisure ideas for Kuwait City attractions, recreation and nightlife
Kuwait City will delight fans of outdoor activities with an abundance of entertainment venues and beautiful places to walk. At every turn you can find attractive shops and markets, huge shopping malls and small souvenir shops. It is a real paradise for shoppers. One of the most famous shopping malls is The Avenues; there are hundreds of shops selling clothes, accessories, jewelry and perfumes in it. Visitors could stroll among glittering display windows all day long. It is almost impossible to leave The Avenues

without buying something, as goods are offered at very attractive prices.

Among the entertainment centers The Scientific is worth visiting, where curious travelers are sure to enjoy. The center has a great aquarium, which introduces a variety of inhabitants of the underwater world to center's guests. There is also a cinema there. In the center there are several science museums, which would be interesting for both children and adults.

The perfect place for strolling is Salmiya district, where the world's most famous pearl market is situated. Here, travelers would have an opportunity to buy unique jewelry. Local pearl divers offer to participate in extracting the precious pearl at a small fee. Fans of beach vacation have to go to the Ras Al-Zour. This scenic piece of coast is well equipped for water sports and is considered one of the most beautiful beaches of the Arabian Gulf.

Those, who prefer outdoor activities, would enjoy an excursion to the island of Al-Siyar. This unspoiled corner of nature dazzles senses; the island is home to a huge number of exotic birds. There is a riding school on the island, so everyone can learn how to stay in the saddle and to explore natural attractions riding a thoroughbred horse.

Among city markets travelers point out the Souk Al-Mubarakiya. Thousands of stalls are offering customers the most diverse goods: beautiful clothes and jewelry, fresh vegetables and fruits, spices and fine national food. Those who hope to bring back from a trip some antiques would also like the market, as there you can find unique antiques. Among other shopping complexes that can attract tourists, Villa Moda, Marina World and the 360 Mall are worth mentioning.

In the capital of Kuwait, be sure to visit Flight Experience in order to get a unique experience of flying a plane. Of course, not a real one, but the impressions promise to be no less exciting. Karting enthusiasts will be able to choose from the two centers for spending a good time - Sirbb Circuit or Pro Kart. Visitors to the city can go ice skating at any time of the year, and hot weather is not a problem. This opportunity is available in Ice Skating Rink where both tourists and locals like to spend time cooling down when it's hot outside. For unforgettable impressions from watching theater performances or interesting concerts, one should go to the Sheikh Jaber Al Ahmad Cultural Center after having previously checked the schedule of upcoming events.

A popular place among tourists and locals alike is Kuwait Zoo whose inhabitants are black and white swans, giraffes, bears, lions, zebras. The zoo is especially recommended to adults traveling in the company of small tourists. And the fact that some of the funny animals can be fed will leave a strong impression, making them happy from the bottom of their heart. Together with the little travelers, it's worth going to another place where you can share a pleasant time with the whole family - KidZania Kuwait. One more interesting place for a big family is the well-styled Cartoon Network World center where kids can frolic in the playground while parents are recharging batteries in a cafe.

Have a great time in Mindmaze Kuwait where visitors can use all their wits and ingenuity to solve interesting riddles. This entertainment center suits best for family fun or spending leisure with friends. Escape quests are also popular, as in the course of the game participants have to put their brain to good use to get out of the room. The most popular escape center is Trapped Inn with its many interesting themed rooms (a pyramid, the knight's castle, a medical laboratory), among which there are several rooms for horror fans. Another escape complex of interest is called Way Out Kuwait. Here they provide rooms themed on space adventures and computer games.

In the city, tourists can find excellent spas where it's nice to relax after an active pastime. For example, Talise Spa with its relaxing atmosphere and Orchid Spa offering very comfortable conditions. Billiards players will not stand aside - they're always welcome in Falcon Billiards Lounge. The city also has a suitable place for those who want to knock down some pins - this is Cozmo Bowling. Since Kuwait is a Muslim country, here there are virtually no bars and clubs that could please those wishing to have a strong drink - facilities of this kind can only be found in the hotels.

Cuisine & restaurants

Cuisine of Kuwait City for gourmets. Places for dinner best restaurants

It's not easy to choose the best one among hundreds of attractive restaurants and cafes of Kuwait City, but some places deserve special attention as they differ much from the rest. The Chocolate Bar is an attractive place. It is a cozy cafe, where guests can taste prefect sweets. Both chocolate lovers and fans of pastries, and those keeping figure would find a suitable dessert here. In addition to cakes and fruit desserts, they offer visitors a refreshing drink, tea and coffee specialties.

The popular Mais Alghanim restaurant offers its guests to taste dishes of Middle Eastern cuisine. Visitors will be able to choose a treat for every taste and budget. Among culinary delights represented, there are rare delicacies and traditional home dishes. Those who can't imagine a meal without their favorite hamburger are welcomed by the Slider Station restaurant. Its menu also provides a decent selection of vegetable salads and light meals. The restaurant also attracts visitors with its reasonable prices.

The Leila restaurant specializes in cooking Lebanese dishes. This establishment has excellent food, pleasant decor and rooms, and attentive staff who will answer all your questions and help to choose dishes. The Leila restaurant is also suitable for celebrations. Excellent restaurant of Japanese cuisine is Kei; every day it is visited by fans of sushi and rolls. Some restaurant's tables are served on the terrace; visitors can also stay in a cozy room decorated in oriental style.

Best pizza and pasta are offered by the Nino restaurant serving Italian cuisine. It is very popular among locals and visitors. Nino is one of the most attractive budget facilities of the city. At their first visit guests may be confused with richly decorated room, but they don't have to overpay for the design, as prices in this restaurant are at moderate level. The One cafe offers a wide selection of international cuisine, in the morning it often serves breakfast in a buffet-style. Its main clients are tourists and employees of nearby offices. The Fauchon restaurant is considered the best in French cuisine. It will also please guests with an amazing interior decoration and delicious treats.

In Kuwait restaurants specializing in regional cuisine, it is customary to begin a meal with traditional appetizers. The most famous among them is Hummus, which is prepared from various types of legumes with the addition of spices and lemon juice. Another popular snack is deep-fried chickpea balls called Falafel.

An important component of local gastronomy is bread, which is baked here in a special oven. Local bread resembles large flat cakes fried to a crisp. Most dishes are traditionally served with "Aish" bread whose name means "life" in Arabic.

Since local people are Muslims, there are no pork dishes in national restaurants. All meat dishes are made from lamb, goat, and veal, often complemented by very interesting vegetable garnishes. In local restaurants, guests will be offered traditional shawarma and dozens of kebab versions, and the most sumptuous festive dish is "Ghouzi" - stuffed lamb.

Poultry meat is used for the preparation of many meat dishes. A great example is "Harees" - a hearty casserole of veal and chicken. An original dish, which is quite cheap in local restaurants, is "Biryani-Dajaj" - stewed chicken with rice. The most common garnish for meat dishes is rice, and Kuwait's chefs have reached incredible heights in the art of its cooking. They use dozens of rice varieties, necessarily adding various spices and vegetables during cooking.

The choice of vegetable dishes in local restaurants is also huge, while stuffed zucchini and eggplants enjoy the greatest popularity among foreign guests. The menu of regional restaurants in Kuwait cannot be imagined without traditional baked goods. In restaurants of various categories, they bake wonderful sambusa patties typically filled with meat, cheese or vegetables. For dessert, local restaurants often serve sweet pastries, including esh-asaya cheesecake, which is characterized by a very original taste. Here you can also taste all kinds of baklava and sherbet, interesting desserts from fresh milk and special types of donuts with honey. Many original sweets can be tasted in street markets.

Traditions & lifestyle

Colors of Kuwait City traditions, festivals, mentality and lifestyle

Kuwait City is a modern bustling city that isn't alien to trends of modern culture. More recently, life there has based on an entirely different traditions and backgrounds. Only some of the important traditions have managed to preserve till these days. The most important aspect of local culture is still the good relationship between family members. The family is considered to be a single entity and a situation, when only one member of the family is invited on some celebration, is simply intolerable. It is a common practice to make visits along with family, whether it is an ordinary trip to visit friends or an important holiday.

Respect and unquestioning obedience to elders is also an important attribute of family relationships. Since childhood, children are taught to help elders and listen to their wise counsel. Seniors, in turn, are required to help the younger members of the family and take part in their lives. Relationships between a man and a woman are also quite distinctive, as they are retired from eyes and considered a taboo subject for discussion. Even legitimate married couples can't walk around in public places, hand in hand, because it is considered a manifestation of bad education and is contrary to religious canons.

Responsibilities of spouses differ: a man should provide material well-being of the family, and a woman has to do housework and to raise children. As it was noted above, each year the impact of modern culture affects lives of citizens more and more, so long, working women are no exception. Locals are very hospitable, they consider it their duty to accept guests adequately and entertain them, so that all were satisfied.

To receive guests there is a special room in each house, which is called 'deevania.' This part of the house is usually separated from the living area and is fully prepared to welcome guests. All that is left to do for hosts is to serve food. Traditionally only men take part in the meal. The invitation to visit is very honorable, so you shouldn't refuse. Local culture is also reflected in the specifics of national costumes, which are very beautiful, and even casual clothing may seem very elegant and solemn to foreigners. Tourists should be sure to learn rules of the local etiquette before the trip, as it will avoid many misunderstandings and would make a vacation comfortable.

Most of the holidays celebrated in the city are of a religious nature. The only exception is Kuwait National Day that falls on February 25. It is timed to the day when the state was declared independent from the British rule in 1961. On the same day, Abdullah Al-Salem Al-Sabah was crowned. Locals are very proud of gaining their independence so noisy parties and celebrations are organized throughout the country. But, of course, the most spectacular actions take place in the capital. Parades, public festivities, theatrical program, the opening of exhibitions, fireworks, national symbols - all this and much more can be seen on February 25 in the central streets of Kuwait City. On this day, it is customary to wear national costumes visit the homes of loved ones and after watching the parades.

Ramadan, the celebration of which falls on the ninth month of the lunar calendar, is the most revered Muslim holiday here. Local residents observe strict fasting throughout the whole month, some restaurants may even refuse to sell alcohol to foreigners. In any case, it is strictly forbidden to drink alcohol in public places during the holy month of Ramadan - if you wish, you can do it at the hotel. At the end of the month, locals celebrate Eid al-Fitr, which translates as "the Day of Breaking the Fast". On this day, "Eid Mubarak!" is heard on the streets, it is customary to perform morning prayer and set a festive table inviting close people to the house. Children are happy at this time: they usually get some tasty sweets. It is also customary to do good deeds for example, to give alms to the poor.

Another holiday widely celebrated in Kuwait is called Qadir-e-Khumm. This one is not really well-known in other Muslim countries, but for Kuwait is of particular importance. People celebrate the event thanks to which Imam Ali became the successor of the Prophet (the latter is revered in a special way in the country). Another holiday associated with Muhammad is Mawlid al-Nabi al-Sharif, which marks the birth of the Prophet. At this time, local people perform solemn prayers and spend time with family and friends, inviting them to dinner. They also celebrate Muhammad's Ascension to Heaven, the holiday is known as Al-Mi'raj.

As well as Hijri New Year, or the Islamic New Year, which marks the beginning of the first month of Muharram. Solemn divine services are held in mosques, locals celebrate the first day in a circle of close people. It is worth noting that throughout the whole month of Muharram, it is strictly forbidden to quarrel with anybody - Muslims avoid even minor conflicts. Throughout the month, believers pray and ask for happiness from Allah for all the good deeds they've done. Another Islamic holiday that is of great importance in Kuwait's religious tradition is Eid al-Adha meaning "the Day of Sacrifice." It is celebrated on the 40th day after Ramadan for three days. It also cannot do without solemn prayers in mosques with the glorification of Allah and Muhammad and talks of the meaning of sacrifice in the Islamic tradition.

Shopping in Kuwait City

Shopping in Kuwait City authentic goods, best outlets, malls and boutiques

Kuwait City is famous for its top-notch shopping centers and markets, and the biggest mall is The Avenues. It is ready to please all comers with luxurious designer boutiques and inexpensive clothing stores, as well as many jewelry salons offering quite attractive prices. Customers will be able to combine shopping with tasting specialties in local restaurants and cafes.

Not far from the pier is Marina Mall, one of the most expensive and prestigious in town. In this complex, you can find boutiques and salons of the most eminent designers like Givenchy. Cafes and restaurants presented here fully correspond to the general level of stores, it is here that one should go to try unique gourmet dishes.

Those who are not expecting to spend huge sums on new outfits would find it more preferable to visit Souq Sharq. This shopping center is one of the busiest in town, characterized by a variety of toy stores and children's products. Here you can also buy affordable clothes from local manufacturers or attend all kinds of festivals and events that will be of interest to the whole family.

Avid fashionistas of both sexes would probably be interested in Villa Moda, one of the most prestigious shopping centers in Kuwait City. It houses a lot of original designer boutiques of both global and local brands where you can buy exclusive clothes and accessories. If one cannot afford luxury goods, they can just walk through the shopping center, which is deservedly considered to be one of the most beautiful in the capital.

Kuwait City has several outlets that will appeal to thrifty travelers, and the most popular one is Olympia Mall. Its visitors will be pleased with the variety of shops, here they can find good casual clothes or elegant business suits, they also sell cosmetics and perfumes in this outlet. Despite its great popularity, Olympia Mall is never crowded, it is always nice to do shopping in a calm and uncrowded atmosphere.

Also, be sure to look through the local markets - Souk Al-Mubarakiya enjoys great popularity among tourists. It presents a wide range of goods in the oriental style: wonderful spices, popular oriental sweets, as well as elegant oriental dresses. Many are attracted to this market by a huge selection of jewelry, which is distinguished by unbelievably attractive prices.

A true attraction of the capital is Fish Market - it would be interesting for tourists to visit it even as part of a regular guided tour. The variety of goods in this market just boggles the mind, here they sell dozens of types of fish, shellfish and other exotic seafood, which cannot be found in any other countries of the world. This market is very popular with local residents - even chefs from local restaurants come here to select the best seafood for their specialties.

A peculiar attraction for Kuwait City is 360 Mall, which is sure to surprise visitors not only with a huge selection of shops but also with its amazing design. Live plants and flowers were used for the shopping center's interior decoration. Spaces between some cafes and recreation areas are separated here by real living walls. The shopping center is known for the abundance of famous European branded stores, it also boasts many specialized shops selling unique products. It will be interesting to walk here in search of cheap souvenirs, and after shopping, one can go to the cinema or recharge batteries in the food court.

Al Hamra Luxury Center will appeal to those who prefer doing shopping in a relaxed and uncrowded atmosphere. High-quality designer clothing, shoes from famous European manufacturers, cosmetics and jewelry, household goods and children's toys are just a few of the product categories that can be found in this mall.

Tips for tourists
Preparing your trip to Kuwait City: advices & hints things to do and to obey

1. Tipping isn't officially accepted, but in some larger restaurants tip may be included in the total account. If you would like to thank the

helpful waiter, you can add to the bill 10% of the amount or to round it up to any convenient sum.

2. Bargaining is possible only at open markets, as bargaining has been a ritual for years and years. In stores and shopping centers commodity prices are fixed; it is also worth noting that there is no VAT in Kuwait.

3. Most shops and malls open at 8:30 - 9:00am and work until 8:00 - 9:00pm. During the day, some stores may be closed for a very long break. Thursday and Saturday are considered short working days, and on Friday almost all shops are closed.

4. Tourists, who are going to call in a lot of other countries and cities, are recommended to purchase a plastic prepaid card. It is sold in all newsstands, petrol stations and post offices. This plastic card is accepted by every payphone. Calls

from conventional street payphones would be the most profitable ones.

5. Travelers, who expect to visit remote areas of the city and travel outside the tourist areas, have to pay attention to the choice of clothes. Clothing for walking should be high-necked and long-sleeved; too bright and provoking attire is considered a sign of bad taste and can be misinterpreted. Tourists in the low-necked clothes don't even receive the permission to enter the territory of religious attractions.

6. Local people are very reluctant to alcoholic beverages; it is possible to consume spirits only in designated areas. The appearance in a public place while being drunk is considered a gross violation of public order, which could be followed by a heavy fine.

7. Main voltage is 220 V; three-pin sockets are most common. Required adapters can be borrowed from the hotel or purchased at any supply store.

8. Banks and other government offices open early, at 7:00-7:30am and serve visitors to 1:00-1:30pm. Some larger agencies may also work for some hours in the evening. Tuesday is a day-off, and Thursday is a half-day.

The Land

Slightly larger in area than the U.S. state of Hawaii, Kuwait is bounded to the west and north by Iraq, to the east by the Persian Gulf, and to the south by Saudi Arabia.

Get unlimited access to all of Britannica's trusted content.Start Your Free Trial Today

Kuwait is largely a desert, except for Al-Jahrā' oasis, at the western end of Kuwait Bay, and a few fertile patches in the southeastern and coastal areas. Kuwaiti territory includes nine offshore islands, the largest of which are the uninhabited Būbiyān and Al-Warbah. The island of Faylakah, which is located near the entrance of Kuwait Bay, has been populated since prehistoric times.

A territory of 2,200 square miles (5,700 square km) along the gulf was shared by Kuwait and Saudi Arabia as a neutral zone until a political boundary was agreed on in 1969. Each of the two countries now administers half of the territory (called the Neutral, or Partitioned, Zone), but they continue to share equally the revenues from oil production in the entire area. Although the boundary with Saudi Arabia is defined, the border with Iraq remains in dispute.

Relief

The relief of Kuwait is generally flat or gently undulating, broken only by occasional low hills and shallow depressions. The elevations range from sea level in the east to 951 feet (290 metres) above sea level at Al-Shiqāyā peak, in the western corner of the country. The Al-Zawr Escarpment, one of the main topographic features, borders the northwestern shore of Kuwait Bay and rises to a maximum elevation of 475 feet (145 metres). Elsewhere in coastal areas, large patches of salty marshland have developed. Throughout the northern, western, and central sections of Kuwait, there are desert basins, which fill with water after winter rains; historically these basins formed important watering places, refuges for the camel herds of the Bedouin.

Drainage

Kuwait has no permanent surface water, either in the form of standing bodies such as lakes or in the form of flows such as perennial rivers. Intermittent water courses (wadis) are localized and generally terminate in interior desert basins. Little precipitation is absorbed beyond the surface level, with most being lost to evaporation.

Soils

True soils scarcely exist naturally in Kuwait. Those that exist are of little agricultural productivity and are marked by an extremely low amount of organic matter. Eolian soils and other sedimentary deposits are common, and a high degree of salinity is found, particularly in basins and other locations where residual water pools. One of the environmental consequences of the

Persian Gulf War was the widespread destruction of the desert's rigid surface layer, which held underlying sand deposits in place; this has led to an increase in wind-borne sand and the creation of larger and more numerous sand dunes in the country.

Climate

The climate is desert, tempered somewhat in the coastal regions by the warm waters of the gulf. If there is enough rainfall, the desert turns green from mid-March to the end of April. But during the dry season, between April and September, the heat is severe daytime temperatures ordinarily reach 111 °F (44 °C) and on occasion approach 130 °F (54 °C). The winter is more agreeable (frost can even occasionally occur in the interior, though never on the seacoast). Annual rainfall averages only from 1 to 7 inches (25 to 180 mm), chiefly between October and

April, though cloudbursts can bring more than 2 inches (50 mm) of rain in a single day.

The frequent winds from the northwest are cool in winter and spring and hot in summer. Southeasterly winds, usually hot and damp, spring up between July and October; hot and dry south winds prevail in spring and early summer. The *shamāl*, a northwesterly wind common during June and July, causes dramatic sandstorms.

Plant and animal life

Except in the new green belt of Kuwait city and in a few desert oases such as Al-Jahrā', where cultivation and irrigation are carried out, the vegetation consists of scrub and low bushes (and ephemeral grass in the spring). Halophytes (salt-loving plants) grow on the marshy stretches along the coast.

The harsh climate limits mammals to the occasional gazelle, fox, or civet. Among lizards are the rare and venomous sand viper (*Cerastes vipera*) and the monitor and vegetarian dab lizards (*Uromastix spinipes*).

The People

Historically, there were several important class divisions in Kuwait. These divisions emerged during the period when the country was a trade entrepôt and were largely economic; thus, as the state became Kuwait's primary employer after oil was discovered in the 1930s and these reserves were commercially developed in subsequent decades, this class structure became less pronounced. The one historically important class that remains politically important is the old merchant oligarchy, the Banū (Banī) ʿUtūb of which the ruling family is a member.

Ethnic groups

Despite a government policy to reduce the number of foreign workers following the Iraqi invasion in 1990, Kuwaitis remain a minority in their own country. About two-thirds of the population are expatriate workers, formerly from other Arab states but now largely from South and Southeast Asia. These nonnationals do not enjoy citizenship rights, economic or political, which are reserved for Kuwaiti citizens defined as those able to prove Kuwaiti ancestry prior to 1920. Naturalization is strictly limited. Arabs either Bedouin, sedentary, or descendants of immigrants from elsewhere in the region constitute the largest ethnic group, and a small number of ethnic Persians have resided in the country for centuries.

Languages

The native and official language is Arabic, fluency in which is a requirement for naturalization. Kuwaitis speak a dialect of Gulf Arabic, and Modern Standard Arabic is taught in schools. English is the second language taught in public schools. Hindi, Urdu, Persian (Farsi), and other languages also are widely spoken among the foreign population.

Religion

Kuwaiti citizens are almost entirely Muslim, and a law passed in 1981 limits citizenship to Muslims. The majority are Sunni, but about one-third are Shīʿite. Both the Iranian revolution of 1979 and the Kuwaiti government's subsequent discrimination against Shīʿites fostered a heightened sense of community among the country's Shīʿite population in the 1980s and '90s, and this led to political tension between the two groups.

Settlement patterns

The old town of Kuwait, although located in a harsh desert climate, opened onto an excellent sheltered harbour. Kuwait developed in the 18th and 19th centuries as a trading city, relying on the pearl banks of the gulf as well as on long-distance sea and caravan traffic. The old city facing the sea and bounded landward from 1918 to 1954 by a mud wall, the gates of which led out into the desert was compact, only 5 square miles (13 square km) in area; its typical dwelling was a courtyard house. After the discovery of oil in the 1930s and the petroleum industry's rapid expansion after World War II, Kuwait city underwent a transformation. The ensuing urban explosion led to the destruction of the semicircular city wall (its gates were preserved as a reminder of the early years), and city planners formally laid out new suburbs. The government invested large portions of oil revenues in infrastructure and urban development, creating in the process a modern metropolis.

Kuwaitis are now scattered at a relatively low density throughout the urban area and surrounding suburbs. Non-Kuwaitis, largely excluded from the restricted suburbs, live at higher densities in the old city and in the suburbs of Ḥawallī and Al-Sālimiyyah, mostly in apartments.

Demographic trends

Until the Iraqi invasion, Palestinians, some of them third-generation residents of Kuwait, were the largest single expatriate group, numbering perhaps 400,000. Popular Palestinian support for Iraq during the war and persistent Palestinian demands for political inclusion led the Kuwaiti government to deport most of them following the restoration of authority, and by early 1992 their number had fallen to 50,000. They have been largely replaced by Egyptians, Syrians, Iranians, and South Asians.

Life expectancy in Kuwait is high, with males living to about 75 years and females to 77. Although Kuwait's birth rate is roughly equal to the world average, its low death rate has led to a high rate of natural increase. The leading cause of death is circulatory disease. The country is young, with roughly one-fourth of the population under the age of 15.

The Economy

Virtually all of Kuwait's wealth is derived directly or indirectly, by way of overseas investments, from petroleum extraction and processing. The most dramatic element of Kuwait's economic development has been the steady and rapid expansion of its oil industry since the 1970s. By the mid-1980s Kuwait was refining four-fifths of its oil domestically and marketing some 250,000 barrels a day in its own European retail outlets under the name "Q8." This oil income and the investment income it generated the latter surpassed direct sales of oil revenues by the 1980s gave Kuwait one of the highest per capita incomes in the world. However, both the Iraqi invasion (which nearly exhausted Kuwait's overseas investment revenues) and the increasing volatility of the global oil market in the 1980s reduced this income substantially, but income levels rebounded when oil prices rose dramatically in the early 21st century. Other sectors of Kuwait's economy are weak by comparison; agriculture, manufacturing, and trade each constituteonly a small proportion of gross domestic product (GDP).

Agriculture and fishing

The possibilities of agricultural development are severely limited. Only a small amount of the land is arable, and, because of scarcity of water, soil deficiencies, and lack of workers trained in agricultural skills, only a portion of that land area is under actual cultivation. Agriculture's contribution, therefore, is insignificant to the output of the economy.

Fish are plentiful in the Persian Gulf, and fishing in Kuwait was a leading industry before the discovery of oil. The United Fisheries of Kuwait continues the tradition today. Shrimp was one of the few commodities besides oil that Kuwait continued to export after World War II. Shrimp production, devastated by the environmental havoc wreaked in the gulf by the Persian Gulf War, had recovered by the mid-1990s.

Resources and power

Kuwait has nearly one-tenth of the world's proven oil reserves. Kuwait's proven recoverable reserves are thought to be enough to sustain current production levels for some 150 years, and, though the oil industry sustained severe damage during the Iraqi invasion, most of that was repaired by the mid-1990s. Kuwait also has considerable natural gas reserves, almost all in the form of associated gas i.e., gas that is produced together with crude oil. There are no other important minerals. Naturally occurring fresh water is scarce; until desalination plants were built after World War II, water had to be imported.

The generation of electricity also has increased significantly as population and industry have grown. Production is concentrated in several large natural-gas–fired power stations, including one at Al-Shuwaykh and another at Al-Shuʻaybah.

Oil

In 1934 the Kuwait Oil Company (KOC), the ownership of which was divided equally between what were then the British Petroleum Company and the Gulf Oil Corporation (of the United States), obtained a concession covering the whole territory except the Neutral Zone. Oil was struck in 1938, but World War II deferred development until 1946. Thereafter, progress was spectacular. In 1953 the American Independent Oil Company and the Getty Oil Company, which jointly held concessions for the Neutral Zone, struck oil in commercial quantities, and in 1955 oil was discovered in northern Kuwait. By 1976 Kuwait had achieved complete control of the KOC, with the former owners retaining the right to purchase at a discount. The government also achieved full ownership of the Kuwait National Petroleum Company (KNPC), which it had formed in 1960 with private Kuwaiti investors. The KNPC, designed to serve as an integrated oil company, controlled the supply and distribution of petroleum products within the country and began marketing operations abroad. In 1980 the government founded the Kuwait Petroleum Corporation as an umbrella organization overseeing the KOC and the KNPC as well as the Kuwait Oil Tanker Company, the Petrochemicals Industries Company, and the Kuwait Foreign Petroleum Exploration Company.

The relatively low cost of oil production in Kuwait stems from certain unique advantages. Most important, there are a number of highly productive wells, the output of which can be varied at short notice, which thus eliminates the need for large numbers of storage tanks. Most of the storage tanks themselves are placed on a ridge set back a few miles from the seacoast at a height of some 300 feet (90 metres); this enables loading operations to be carried out by gravity rather than by pumps. There are also extensive refineries and bunkers for tankers. While retreating from Kuwait at the end of the Persian Gulf War, Iraqi forces set fire to more than 700 of the country's 950 wells. By the fall of 1991, the fires, which had consumed about six million barrels of oil per day, had been extinguished, and production soon returned to preinvasion levels.

Natural gas

Massive volumes of natural gas are produced in association with crude oil. Although natural gas has great potential as a source of foreign exchange, it principally has been used for reinjection in oil fields to maintain pressure, generating electricity (notably for water distillation), and producing (as raw material) petrochemicals and fertilizers, some of which Kuwait exports in small quantities.

Water

For fresh water in earlier days, people depended on a few artesian wells and on rainwater collected from the roofs of houses or from cisterns at ground level. Dhows piloted by Kuwaiti seamen also brought fresh water from the Shatt al-Arab near Al-Baṣrah, Iraq. With the rapid growth of population, however, the government of Kuwait built desalination plants at Kuwait city, Al-Shuʿaybah, and several other locations. Important sources of fresh water have been discovered at Al-Rawḍatayn and Al-Shiqāyā, but desalination still provides the great bulk of Kuwait's daily consumption of potable water.

Manufacturing

Manufacturing contributes roughly one-tenth of Kuwait's GDP and consists almost entirely of refined petroleum products, petrochemicals, and fertilizers. Other, less-important manufactured products include clothing and apparel, fabricated metal products, industrial chemicals, and nonelectrical machinery.

Finance

The Central Bank of Kuwait (Bank al-Kuwayt al-Markazī) issues the national currency, the Kuwaiti dinar, and is the country's main banking regulatory body. In addition to its central bank, Kuwait has specialized banks operating in the areas of savings and credit, industrial loans, and real estate. There are also commercial banks. No foreign banks may operate in Kuwait, with the exception of the Bank of Bahrain and Kuwait, based in Bahrain and owned equally by the two states. An Islamic bank one bound by stringent religious laws governing financial transactions has also been established. Before independence an officially sanctioned stock exchange operated, growing to become one of the largest in the world. The fall of the unofficial but wildly popular stock market, the Sūq al-Manākh, in 1982 sent the local economy into a mild recession. A resulting debt-settlement program supervised by the government was not completed until the early 21st century. The official Kuwait Stock Exchange was established in 1977.

Trade

Petroleum and petroleum-derived products account for all but a very minor portion of Kuwait's exports, with Asia and the Middle East being the most important markets. Kuwait's imports largely machinery and transport equipment, manufactured goods, and food are principally from China, the United States, Japan, and countries of the European Union.

Services

Kuwait has invested only marginally in local industry. As a result, nearly all employed Kuwaitis work for the state, largely in education (only a small fraction of these are in the oil industry). Almost one-third of the government's revenues are spent on salaries. Tourism plays only a small role in the country's economy. The Iraqi invasion further limited its importance, and the sector has been slow to recover.

Labour and taxation

In both the public and private sectors, Kuwait remains heavily dependent on foreign labour, despite repeated reforms aimed at reducing this dependency. By the late 1990s only one-fifth of the country's workforce were Kuwaiti nationals;

of that number, more than one-third were women. Trade unions are allowed, but numerous restrictions limit their establishment. Less than one-tenth of the country's workforce belongs to a union.

Kuwait has no individual income tax. Much of the government's revenue comes from oilas well as from taxes on foreign corporations and on the foreign interests of Kuwaiti companies.

Transportation and telecommunications

Although there are no railways in the country, Kuwait has a modern road system linking it with its neighbours, as well as a large international airport, Kuwait International Airport, which is located just south of the capital. Kuwait Airways Corporation, a state-owned enterprise, serves a number of international routes. The country's port facilities and its fleet of oil tankers and general cargo ships have been expanded.

Regular telephone service was established in Kuwait only in the 1950s; since that time the country has made significant progress in telephone, cable, wireless communication, and Internet service. The country's communication infrastructure was badly damaged during the Iraqi invasion, but the damage has largely been repaired, and the Kuwaiti government through its Ministry of Communications has further developed Kuwait's communication grid by means of contracts with international telecommunications firms.

Government And Society

Constitutional framework

Kuwait is a constitutional monarchy with one legislative body. Since gaining independence from Britain in 1961, Kuwait has been governed by an emir from the Ṣabāḥ family. The emir rules through a Council of Ministers consisting largely of members of his own family that he himself appoints. Legislative power rests in the National Assembly (Majlis al-Ummah), whose 50 members are elected to four-year terms. This parliament, however, was suspended in 1976, in 1985, and again in 1999.

Justice

Kuwait's legal system has several sources. Personal and civil law (roughly, family law and probate law) are based largely on Sharīʿah (Islamic law). Commercial and criminal law, while also influenced by Sharīʿah, borrows heavily from both European civil and common law as well as from the legal codes of the Ottoman Empire and from those of other Arab states, which are themselves heavily influenced by European law.

There are several lower courts and a system of appeals courts. The emir sometimes acts as the final court of appeal.

Political process

In lieu of political parties, which are prohibited in Kuwait, several quasi-political organizations have representatives in the parliament. For a number of years, voting was limited to natural-born Kuwaiti men who were at least 21 years old; servicemen, police, and women were barred from voting. Under these qualifications, approximately one-tenth of the population formed the electorate. Beginning in the 1990s, attempts to extend suffrage to women increased. In 1999 the emir announced that he would allow women to vote in future elections; the franchise was officially granted in 2005, and in 2009 women were elected to parliament for the first time.

Security

Kuwait's military expenditure per capita is among the highest in the world. Such spending is largely a result of the hostile relationship with Iraq; after the Persian Gulf War, Kuwait undertook significant measures to modernize and increase its armed forces. U.S. troops have been stationed there since the early 1990s, and Kuwait also has defense agreements with other countries, including Russia, the United Kingdom, and France. Kuwaiti males are required to serve two years in the armed forces, although university students may receive exemptions for one year of that service.

Health and welfare

Kuwait has a comprehensive scheme of social welfare. The needy receive financial assistance; loans are provided to the handicapped to start businesses; the disabled can get treatment and training; and education is available for adult illiterates. The Ministry of Social Affairs offers a program that provides adequate, affordable housing, fully equipped with modern facilities, for citizens with limited incomes. Kuwait also has a comprehensive and highly developed subsidized national health-care system. In 1976 the government established Kuwait's Reserve Fund for Future Generations, and it has set aside 10 percent of the state's revenues annually for it. The government found it necessary, however, to tap into that fund during the Iraqi occupation.

Housing

Housing in Kuwait is heavily subsidized by the government, and since the government has invested large amounts of money in development since the oil boom housing standards are generally high. Traditional housing (mud-walled structures one to two stories tall) has largely given way to modern-style homes and apartment complexes in most parts of the country.

Education

About four-fifths of the population is literate. General education in Kuwait is compulsory for native Kuwaitis between the ages of 6 and 14. It is entirely free and also includes school meals, books, uniforms, transportation, and medical attention. Non-Kuwaiti students typically attend private schools. Kuwait University was founded in 1964. The vast majority of its students are Kuwaitis, and about three-fifths are women. In 2001 the university began segregating by gender, a move that was called for by the National Assembly. Other institutions of higher learning include the College of Technological Studies. The American University of Kuwait was established in

2004. Several thousand students attend colleges and universities overseas, principally in the United States, Britain, and Egypt, usually on state scholarships.

Cultural Life

Although Kuwait embraces many facets of Western culture, the country remains culturally conservative. Its Arab-Islamic heritage permeates daily life. As in much of the Middle East, the rise of Islamic fundamentalism in the 1970s and '80s was reflected in a general return to traditional customs, as seen in the public dress of women, who began wearing the *ḥijāb*, or veil, far more than in the past. The right of women to drive automobiles and to work outside the home is generally accepted and has not been a matter of public debate, yet the question of granting women the right to vote has divided Islamists, some of whom seek to enforce even more conservative Islamic standards such as those found in neighbouring Saudi Arabia.

Daily life and social customs

At the heart of traditional Kuwaiti culture is the institution of the *diwāniyyah*, a regular gathering of men usually in a tent or a separate room of the main house which serves as a time to gather, enjoy refreshments, talk, or play games. Kuwaitis observe all major Islamic holidays, including Ramadan and the two *ʿīd*s (festivals), ʿĪd al-Fiṭr and ʿĪd al-Aḍḥā. The country's Independence Day and Liberation Day (from the Iraqi occupation of 1990–91) are important secular holidays.

Fūl, falafel, and hummus are the cornerstones of Kuwaiti cuisine, though Western fast-food restaurants abound in Kuwait city. *Fūl* is a paste based on fava beans, with garlic and lemon added. Formed from fried balls of chickpeas and spices, falafel is often served in unleavened bread (*khubz*) with vegetables. Chickpeas are also used to make hummus, a dip for vegetables and bread. The traditional Kuwaiti meal consists of spiced rice topped with meat or fish or shellfish taken from the Persian Gulf.

The arts

Kuwaiti folk arts remain important, and Bedouin crafts are the most prominent. Though few Bedouins now inhabit Kuwait, their art traditions, especially weaving, have been maintained. The intricately woven fabrics are made on a *sadu*, a Bedouin loom, and are common sights in souks (bazaars). Sadu House, a museum for Bedouin crafts, offers classes on weaving. Also popular are traditional dances, including the *'arḍah*, which features swords and poetry singing. The government supports the preservation of folk arts and funds numerous organizations, as well as several troupes that perform across the country.

Cultural institutions

Kuwait has numerous museums, but the Iraqi invasion had a disastrous effect on many institutions. Many artworks were stolen by the Iraqis, and some buildings were severely damaged. The National Museum of Kuwait, which once housed a comprehensivecollection of Islamic art, was looted and set ablaze; only a small portion of the building has been renovated and reopened to the public. The loss increased the importance of the Tareq Rajab Museum (Maṭḥaf Ṭāriq), a private collection that features paintings, pottery, metalwork, jewelry, and musical instruments, among other items. The Seif Palace which was built in 1910 and later underwent numerous renovations and repairs is one of the ruling family's official residences and is a popular tourist attraction noted for its Islamic architecture.

Sports and recreation

Kuwait's sports culture, like that of other gulf states, combines the traditional sports of nomadic Arabian society with contemporary sports of Western origin. Traditional sports of enduring popularity include camel and horse racing; Arabian horses are held to be among the finest in the world. Falconry is enjoyed primarily by wealthy sheikhs, although the overhunting of game and, after 1990, the presence of unexploded land mines in the desert have reduced its practice. Kuwaitis have competed at the national and international levels in the country's two most widely played sports, football (soccer) and golf. Oil revenues have enabled the government to support sports generously, and the country boasts a number of stadiums capable of hosting international competitions. The country first participated in the 1968 Summer Olympic Games, but it has never competed at the Winter Games.

Media and publishing

The Ministry of Information runs the government press and the radio and television broadcasting stations. Much of the print media receives financial support from the government. Although the constitution guarantees freedom of the press, this right has often been suspended. In 1992 print restrictions were relaxed on the condition that the media sources monitor themselves. Direct criticism of the emir, however, is still prohibited.

History

Strategic importance

At the time of the Iraqi invasion of Kuwait in
1990, there was some speculation, in Western
countries at least, as to why such an
unprepossessing splinter of desert should be
worth the trouble. Of course, anyone watching
the retreating Iraqi army, under skies black from
burning wells, could find an easy answer: oil. But
oil was only half of the story. Kuwait is not, nor
has it ever been, simply a piece of oil-rich desert.
Rather, it represents a vital (in all senses of the
word) piece of coast that for centuries has
provided settlement, trade and a strategic
staging post. The latter is a point not lost on US
military forces, who until recently camped out on
Failaka Island. A decade ago, the same island, at
the mouth of Kuwait Bay, was occupied by the
Iraqis. Roughly 2300years before that, it was the
turn of the ancient Greeks, attracted to one of

only two natural harbours in the Gulf; and 2000 years earlier still, it belonged to the great Dilmun empire, based in Bahrain. The country has a curious way of cleaning up history once the protagonists have departed, and just as there's very little evidence of recent events without some determined (and ill-advised) unearthing, the same could be said of the rest of Kuwait's 10, 000 years of history.

Early history

Standing at the bottom of Mutla Ridge on the road to Bubiyan Island, and staring across the springtime grasslands at the estuary waters beyond, it's easy enough to imagine why Stone Age man chose to inhabit the area around Ras Subiyah, on the northern shores of Kuwait Bay. Here the waters are rich in silt from the mighty river systems of southern Iraq, making for abundant marine life. Evidence of the first proper settlement in the region dates from 4500 BC, and shards of pottery, stone walls, tools, a small drilled pearl and remains of what is perhaps the world's earliest seafaring boat indicate links with the Ubaid people who populated ancient Mesopotamia. The people of Dilmun also saw the potential of living in the mouth of two of the world's great river systems and built a large town on Failaka Island, the remains of which form some of the best structural evidence of Bronze Age life in the world.

The greeks on failaka island

A historian called Arrian, in the time of Alexander the Great, first put the region on the map by referring to an island discovered by one of Alexander's generals en route to India. Alexander himself is said to have called this, the modern-day island of Failaka, Ikaros, and it soon lived up to its Greek name as a Hellenistic settlement that thrived between the 3rd and 1st centuries BC. With temples dedicated to Artemis and Apollo, an inscribed stele with instructions to the inhabitants of this high-flying little colonial outpost, stashes of silver Greek coins, busts and decorative friezes, Ikaros became an important trading post on the route from Mesopotamia to India. While there is still a column or two standing proud among the weeds, and the odd returning Kuwaiti trying to resettle amid the barbed wire, there's little left to commemorate the vigorous trading in pearls and incense by the Greeks. There's even less to show for the Christian community that settled among the ruins thereafter.

Growth of kuwait city

Over time, Kuwait's main settlements shifted from island to mainland. In AD 500 the area around Ras Khazimah, near Al-Jahra, was the main centre of population, and it took a further 1200 years for the centre of activity to nudge along the bay to Kuwait City. When looking at the view from the top of the Kuwait Towers, it's hard to imagine that 350 years ago this enormous city was comprised of nothing more illustrious than a few Bedouin tents clustered around a storehouse-cum-fort. Like a tide, its population swelled in the intense summer heat as nomadic families drifted in from the bone-dry desert and then receded as the winter months stretched good grazing across the interior.

Permanent families living around the fort became able and prosperous traders. One such family, Al-Sabah, whose descendants now rule Kuwait, assumed responsibility for local law and order, and under their governance, the settlement grew quickly. By 1760, when the town's first wall was built, the community had a distinctive character. It was comprised of merchant traders, centred around a dhow and ocean-going boon fleet of 800 vessels, and a craft-oriented internal trade, arising from the camel caravans plying the route from Baghdad and Damascus to the interior of the Arabian Peninsula.

Relations with the british

By the early 19th century, as a thriving trading port, Kuwait City was well in the making. However, trouble was always quite literally just over the horizon. There were pirates marauding the waters of the Arabian coast; Persians snatched Basra in the north; various Arab tribes from the west and south had their own designs; and then, of course, there were the ubiquitous Ottomans. Though the Kuwaitis generally got on well with the Ottomans, official Kuwaiti history is adamant that the sheikhdom always remained independent of them, and it is true that as the Turks strengthened their control of eastern Arabia (then known as Al-Hasa), the Kuwaitis skilfully managed to avoid being absorbed by the empire. Nonetheless, Al-Sabah emirs accepted the nominal Ottoman title of 'Provincial Governors of Al-Hasa'.

Enter the British. The Kuwaitis and the British were natural allies in many regards. From the 1770s the British had been contracted to deliver mail between the Gulf and Aleppoin Syria. Kuwait, meanwhile, handled all the trans-shipments of textiles, rice, coffee, sugar, tobacco, spices, teak and mangrove to and from India, and played a pivotal role in the overland trade to the Mediterranean. The British helped to stop the piracy that threatened the seafaring trade, but were not in a position to repel the Ottoman incursions that is until the most important figure in Kuwait's modern history stepped onto the stage.

Sheikh Mubarak al-Sabah al-Sabah, commonly known as Mubarak the Great (r 1896–1915), was deeply suspicious that Constantinople planned to annex Kuwait. Concerned that the emir was sympathetic towards the Ottomans, he killed him, not minding he was committing fratricide as well as regicide, and installed himself as ruler. Crucially, in 1899, he signed an agreement with Britain: in exchange for the British navy's protection, he promised not to give territory to, take support from or negotiate with any other foreign power without British consent. The Ottomans continued to claim sovereignty over Kuwait, but they were now in no position to enforce it. For Britain's part, Prussia, the main ally and financial backer of Turkey, was kept out of the warm waters of the Gulf and trade continued as normal.

Rags to riches in the 20th century

Mubarak the Great laid down the foundations of a modern state. Under his reign, government welfare programmes provided for public schools and medical services. In1912, postal and telegraphic services were established, and water-purification equipment was imported for the American Mission Hospital. According to British surveys from this era, Kuwait City numbered 35, 000 people, with 3000 permanent residents, 500 shops and three schools, and nearly 700 pearling boats employing 10, 000 men.

In the 1920s a new threat in the guise of the terrifying *ikhwan* (brotherhood) came from the Najd, the interior of Arabia. This army of Bedouin warriors was commanded by Abdul Aziz bin

Abdul Rahman al-Saud (Ibn Saud), the founder of modern Saudi Arabia. Despite having received hospitality from the Kuwaitis during his own years in the wilderness, so to speak, he made no secret of his belief that Kuwait belonged to the new kingdom of Saudi Arabia. The Red Fort, currently being restored at Al-Jahra, was the site of a famous battle in which the Kuwaitis put up a spirited defence. They also hurriedly constructed a new city wall, the gates of which can be seen today along Al-Soor St in Kuwait City. In 1923 the fighting ended with a British-brokered treaty under which Abdul Aziz recognised Kuwait's independence, but at the price of two-thirds of the emirate's territory.

The Great Depression that sunk the world into poverty coincided with the demise of Kuwait's pearling industry as the market became flooded with Japanese cultured pearls. At the point when the future looked most dire for Kuwait, however, an oil concession was granted in 1934 to a US-British joint venture known as the Kuwait Oil Company (KOC). The first wells were sunk in 1936 and by 1938 it was obvious that Kuwait was virtually floating on oil. WWII forced KOC to suspend its operations, but when oil exports took off after the war, Kuwait's economy was launched on an unimaginable trajectory of wealth.

In 1950, Sheikh Abdullah al-Salem al-Sabah (r 1950–65) became the first 'oil sheikh'. His reign was not, however, marked by the kind of profligacy with which that term later came to be associated. As the country became wealthy, health care, education and the general standard of living improved dramatically. In 1949 Kuwait had only four doctors; by 1967 it had 400.

Independence

On 19 June 1961, Kuwait became an independent state and the obsolete agreement with Britain was dissolved by mutual consent. In an act of foreboding, the President of Iraq, Abdulkarim Qasim, immediately claimed Kuwait as Iraqi territory. British forces, later replaced by those of the Arab League (which Kuwait joined in 1963), faced down the challenge, but the precedent was not so easily overcome.

Elections for Kuwait's first National Assembly were held in 1962. Although representatives of the country's leading merchant families won the bulk of the seats, radicals had a toehold in the parliament from its inception. Despite the democratic nature of the constitution and the broad guarantees of freedoms and rights including freedom of conscience, religion and press, and equality before the law the radicals immediately began pressing for faster social change, and the country changed cabinets three times between 1963 and 1965. In August 1976 the cabinet resigned, claiming that the assembly had made day-to-day governance impossible, and the emir suspended the constitution and dissolved the assembly. It wasn't until 1981 that the next elections were held, but then parliament was dissolved again in 1986. In December 1989 and January1990 an extraordinary series of demonstrations took place calling for the restoration of the 1962 constitution and the reconvening of parliament.

The invasion of iraq

Despite these political and economic tensions, by early 1990 the country's economic prospects looked bright, particularly with an end to the eight-year Iran–Iraq War, during which time Kuwait had extended considerable support to

Iraq. In light of this, the events that followed were all the more shocking to most people in the region. On 16 July 1990, Iraq sent a letter to the Arab League accusing Kuwait of exceeding its Organization of Petroleum Exporting Countries (OPEC) quota and of stealing oil from the Iraqi portion of an oilfield straddling the border. The following day Iraqi president Saddam Hussein hinted at military action. The tanks came crashing over the border at 2am on 2 August and the Iraqi military was in Kuwait City before dawn. By noon they had reached the Saudi frontier. The Kuwaiti emir and his cabinet fled to Saudi Arabia.

On 8 August, Iraq annexed the emirate. Western countries, led by the USA, began to enforce a UN embargo on trade with Iraq, and in the months that followed more than half a million foreign troops amassed in Saudi Arabia. On 15 January, after a deadline given to Iraq to leave Kuwait had lapsed, Allied aircraft began a five-week bombing campaign nicknamed 'Desert Storm'. The Iraqi army quickly crumbled and on 26 February 1991, Allied forces arrived in Kuwait City to be greeted by jubilant crowds and by clouds of acrid black smoke from oil wells torched by the retreating Iraqi army. Ignoring demands to retreat unarmed and on foot, a stalled convoy of Iraqi armoured tanks, cars and trucks trying to ascend Mutla Ridge became the target of a ferocious Allied attack, nicknamed 'the turkey shoot'.

Physical signs of the Iraqi invasion are hard to find in today's Kuwait. Gleaming shopping malls, new hotels and four-lane highways are all evidence of Kuwait's efforts to put the destruction behind it. However, the emotional scars have yet to be healed, particularly as hundreds of missing prisoners of war are yet to be accounted for, despite the fall of Saddam Hussein.

Kuwait after the demise of saddam hussein

In March 2003 the Allied invasion of Iraq threw the country into paralysing fear of a return to the bad old days of 1990, and it was only with the death of Saddam Hussein (he was hanged on 30 December 2006) that Kuwaitis have finally been able to sigh with relief. Without having to look over its shoulder constantly, Kuwait has lost no time in forging ahead with its ambitious plans, including that of attracting a greater number of regional tourists. The annual Hala Shopping Festival in February is proving a successful commercial venture, attracting visitors from across the region, and resorts offer R&R mostly to the international business community. More significantly, cross-border trade with Iraq (particularly of a military kind) has helped fuel the economic boom of the past five years.

The End

Made in the USA
Columbia, SC
04 September 2021

44816984R00074